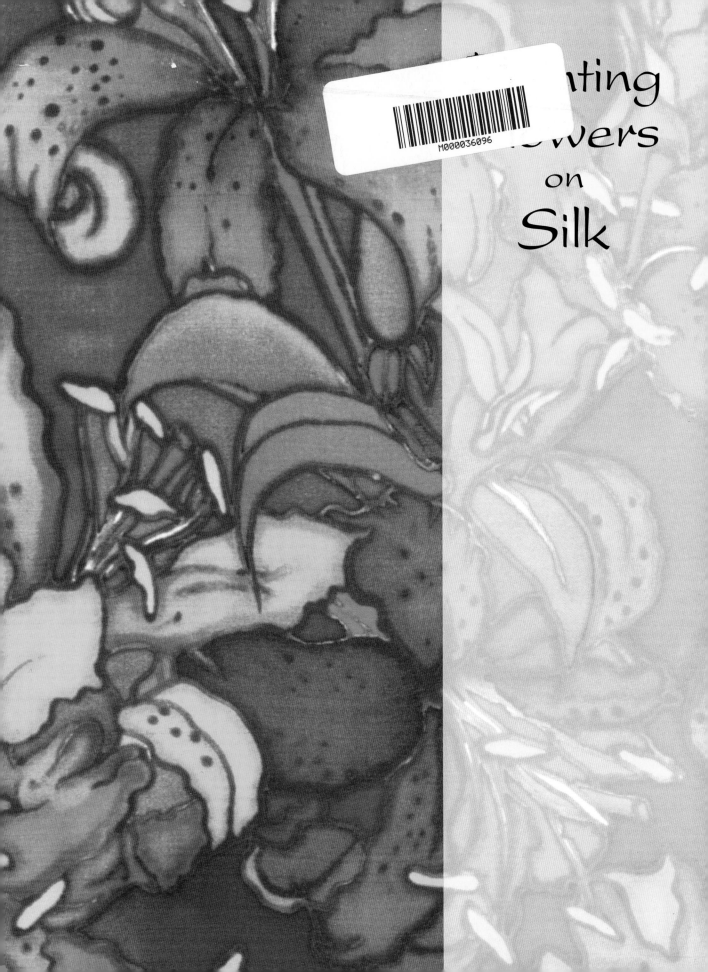

ating
wers

on

Silk

For my parents

Painting
Flowers
on
Silk

Mandy Southan

SEARCH PRESS

First published in Great Britain 2000

Search Press Limited
Wellwood, North Farm Road,
Tunbridge Wells, Kent TN2 3DR

Text copyright © Mandy Southan 2000

Photographs by Search Press Studios
Photographs and design copyright © Search Press Ltd. 2000

ISBN 0 85532 901 7

Suppliers
If you have difficulty in obtaining any of the materials and
equipment mentioned in this book, then please visit the
Search Press website for details of suppliers:
www.searchpress.com

Alternatively, you can write to the Publishers at the address
above, for a current list of stockists, which includes firms who
operate a mail-order service.

Publishers' note
All the step-by-step photographs in this book feature
the author, Mandy Southan, demonstrating how to
paint flowers on silk. No models have been used.

Colour separation by Graphics '91 Pte Ltd, Singapore
Printed in Spain by Elkar S. Coop. Bilbao 48012

*Special thanks to my husband,
Ian, and my children, Jenny,
Ben and Jack, for their love and
patience while I have been
immersed in flowers and silk
over the past year.*

*I would also like to thank
everyone at Search Press,
especially Chantal Roser for her
sensitive and skilful editing,
Julie Wood for her imaginative
design work, and Lotti de la
Bédoyère for her excellent
photography – it has been a
pleasure working with them.*

*Thank you also to all my
students who constantly refire
my enthusiasm for painting and
teaching.*

*Lastly, I would like to thank all
my family and friends for the
happiness they have given me.*

Page 1 Tiger lilies
*The violet outlines in this
painting are made by mixing
violet dye with thickener
(epaississant) – this is not a true
resist but it is effective as long as
you do not make the painting
too wet!*

Pages 2–3 Anemones
*These anemones are painted
with dyes mixed with thickener
to prevent the colours from
spreading.*

Pages 4–5 Amaryllis scarf
*This pretty silk georgette scarf is
painted using wax to partially
define the amaryllis flowers, and
diffusing medium to stripe the
petals and leaves.*

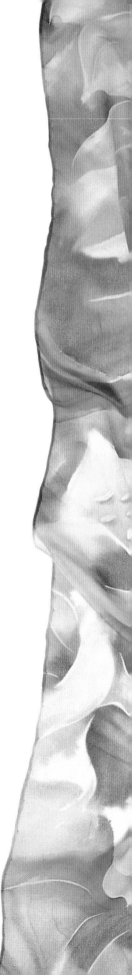

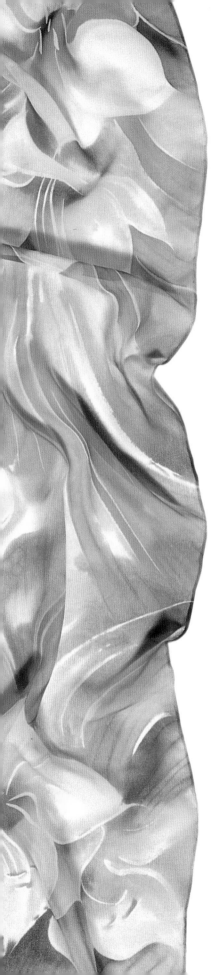

Contents

Introduction

When I was asked to write a book on painting flowers on silk, I knew it would be a wonderful project to work on. I adore all flowers – cultivated, wild and exotic – and I also love painting on silk, so the chance to combine my interests was irresistible!

I am constantly amazed by the complexity of design in nature, and I find the diversity of colours and shapes in flowers an endless source of inspiration for my paintings and textile designs. Silk is a wonderful surface to work on, and a number of intriguing techniques can be used to achieve unusual effects, providing new possibilities for flower painters. I work with steam-fix silk dyes as they are easy to use and the colours are very pure, making it easy to achieve clear and vibrant flowers.

In this book I have painted some of my favourite flowers as step-by-step projects using a variety of techniques to illustrate the breadth and diversity of the medium. I have included designs so you can copy the projects, or you may prefer to use the methods and ideas shown to paint your own flowers. Remember, there is no 'one way' or 'right way' to paint flowers. You can use any of the techniques covered in this book, and each will achieve completely different results. Think about what you want to express in your painting before you start, then consider which technique might best convey what you feel about the flower or flowers you have chosen.

All the projects can be painted on a 50 x 50cm (19½ x 19½in) frame (there will be a little surplus silk around some designs), or you can use an adjustable frame to get the exact inside measurement, as given for each project. You can also adapt the projects for larger pieces if you like!

I have included a section on colour mixing, as I am aware that many people find this difficult. All the colours in the projects are mixed from six basic colours (see page 12). The basic colours required for each project are given in the *You Will Need* lists.

I have taught painting on silk for many years, and I have found that the majority of my students love painting flowers. Beginners are fascinated to discover how the dyes spread and fill the spaces outlined with resists, and are excited by the wonderful colours they can mix. As confidence and experience grow, students try other techniques, and start to experiment further, allowing the medium to offer its own unique magic.

If you have no artistic experience, do not be deterred – you will be amazed by what you can achieve very quickly. If you are already an experienced flower painter, but are used to working on paper, you will probably be captivated when you try painting flowers on silk. Even if you already paint flowers on silk, I am sure this book will give you some new ideas. Whatever your level of artistic ability, I hope the following pages will add a little fertiliser to your creative soil!

***French flowers**
French flower markets are a delight! Bunches of mixed flowers are arranged in wonderful combinations of colours. These flowers were painted freely directly on to dry silk. A little clear gutta was used to define the centres of the daisies.*

Materials

A comprehensive selection of materials is featured in this section, but you do not need all this to begin silk painting – all you need is a frame, a piece of silk, a brush and a few basic colours. A list of materials required accompanies each project, but in addition you will need jars of clean water, paper towelling, palettes and droppers.

Silk

Different types are available for painting, and each produces different results. I have specified which silk I have used for each project.

Steam-fix silk dyes

These are very versatile and easy to work with. The colours are vibrant and can be manipulated on the silk to achieve beautiful textural effects unique to silk painting.

Droppers

These are used for transferring dyes from bottles to a palette.

Discharge dyes and illuminants

These are special dyes used in the discharge technique. Dyes which can be bleached out of the silk with a reducing agent (discharge salt) are 'dischargeable'. Dyes which are unaffected by a reducing agent are called 'illuminants'. They are used to replace a discharged area with another colour.

Brushes

Foam, mop, flat and round brushes are all useful. You will need a variety of sizes. Soft-haired, springy brushes with good points are easiest to work with. Brushes should be washed in warm water with a little soap to remove surplus dye from under the ferrule. Rinse and dry them carefully, reshaping the hairs into a point.

Palette

An ice cube tray makes an excellent palette, and a porcelain or plastic watercolour palette can also be used. If you are working on large pieces, use a palette with deep wells so that it will hold plenty of dye, or use small jars.

Resists and applicators

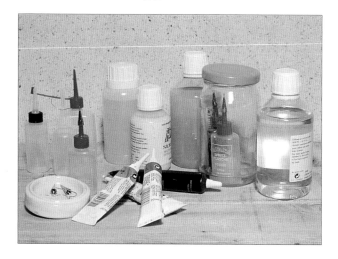

Clear water-based gutta is available in tubes and jars. Water-based gutta is washed out of the silk after fixing. It forms a reasonable resist but will not stand up to repeated overpainting.

Clear spirit-based gutta is a liquid latex rubber which forms an excellent resist. Fine lines can be left in the silk or removed after fixing by dry-cleaning or by rinsing in white spirit.

Spirit-based gutta can be stored in a **screw-top jar** containing a little **white spirit** to stop it evaporating and thickening.

Essence 'F' is a spirit sold with spirit-based gutta to thin it to the correct consistency – that of runny honey.

Coloured guttas and **metallic outliners** are available in many different colours. You can buy them in tubes or jars.

You can transfer gutta into a **gutta bottle** fitted with a **gutta nib**. Gutta nibs come in different widths – fine ones for fine line work, and larger ones for metallic outliners and broad outlines.

Gutta wire is used to seal the fine spout of the gutta nib when not in use. It prevents the gutta from drying and blocking the nib. It is not stiff enough to use to unblock a spout – you should use a fine needle instead.

Special effect materials

Etching gel is a chemical which dissolves cellulose. It is used on viscose/silk mixes such as velvet to create a devoré design. It 'burns out' the viscose pile whilst leaving the silk backing intact.

Anti-spread medium is used to treat the silk so that the dyes will not spread when they are applied. You can also make your own anti-spread by mixing thickener with water.

Diffusing medium is a levelling agent which can be mixed with the dyes to help them spread and blend evenly on the silk. It can also be used instead of water to create tints of colours. It can be applied over painted areas to create interesting marks and textures.

Coarse salt such as rock or sea salt will make bold patterns when sprinkled on to damp painted silk. **Fine salt** makes more delicate patterns.

Discharge salt is a reducing agent which bleaches out colour.

Thickener can be mixed with dyes or discharge salt and illuminants to prevent the colours from spreading. It can also be mixed with a little dye and used as a coloured water-based gutta, or mixed with water to treat the silk to produce an anti-spread surface.

Wax equipment

An **electric wax pot** is used to melt wax. It is thermostatically controlled to keep the melted wax at the correct temperature.

General purpose **batik wax granules** are melted down in the wax pot and used as a resist. They can be purchased from craft shops and silk painting and candle maker's suppliers. Cheaper paraffin wax can also be used.

Tjantings are brass- or copper-bowled Javanese tools with fine spouts. They are used to draw the melted wax on to the silk.

A natural-haired **brush** is used to paint on the melted wax.

An **iron** is used for ironing out wax and for removing creases from finished pieces. Protect your ironing board with a clean cotton cloth or newspaper.

Old newspapers or clean newsprint are used when ironing out wax. Do not use fresh newspapers, as these can transfer ink to the silk.

Paper towelling is used for wiping brushes and removing surplus dye from waxed areas.

Other materials

Silk is pinned to a **frame** to prevent it from touching your work surface as you paint it. Wooden and plastic ones are available in various adjustable designs. The frame needs to be the size of the piece of silk you are working on.

Three-point silk pins or **stenter pins** and **rubber bands** are used to attach silk to the frame. The latter are particularly useful for pinning silk with pre-rolled edges and for silk velvet. You should re-tension the silk as necessary as you are working, so that the dye dries evenly.

Designs can be raised under the silk on a **board**, and protected with **polythene**.

You can draw on to silk with an **autofade marker**. The lines will fade automatically after a few hours or when dye or water is applied. A **soft graphite or charcoal pencil** can also be used for drawing on to the silk – use lightly, as heavy line work will show up in the finished painting.

A **water mister** is used for damping the silk.

Silk can be cut with **scissors** or nicked and then torn on the grain.

Brushes should be rinsed in a **water jar**. Have at least two jars of water beside you as you work and keep one clean for mixing colours.

A **hairdryer** is used to dry dye and gutta.

Plastic gloves should be worn to protect hands from dye stains and chemicals.

Using colour

Good colour mixing is important when painting flowers, perhaps more so than for any other subject. There is nothing more frustrating than trying to capture the beautiful violet of a pansy but only managing to mix a dirty brown or grey!

For many painters, however, colour mixing can be a confusing business. The most important thing is to select the correct colours to start with and to be able to identify the difference between them.

Basic colours

I use a small range of six basic colours: orangey yellow, greeny yellow, greeny blue, violety blue, violety red and orangey red. These can be intermixed to produce a virtually endless range of colours.

All the projects in this book list only the basic blues, reds and yellows needed, and from these you will need to mix up the other colours before you begin the project.

1	2		3	4		5	6
orangey yellow (golden)	greeny yellow (lemon)		greeny blue (cyan)	violety blue (ultramarine)		violety red (magenta)	orangey red (vermilion)

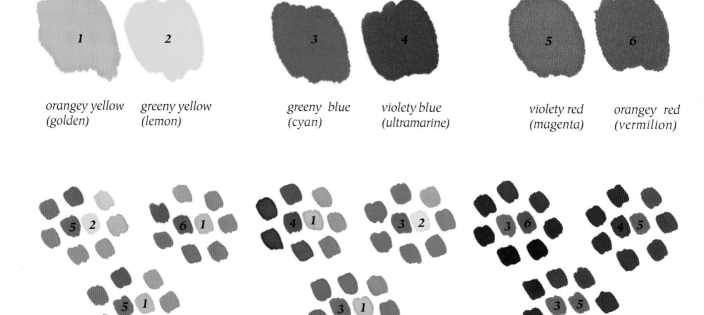

Yellows and reds can be mixed together to make oranges

Yellows and blues can be mixed together to make greens

Blues and reds can be mixed together to make violets

Complementary colours

When the colours of the spectrum are arranged in a circle (a colour wheel) the complementary colours are found opposite each other: oranges and blues; greens and reds; violets and yellows. These complementary 'pairs' of colours are very important in painting and can be used to create many different effects (see pages 14–15).

oranges and blues   *greens and reds*   *violets and yellows*

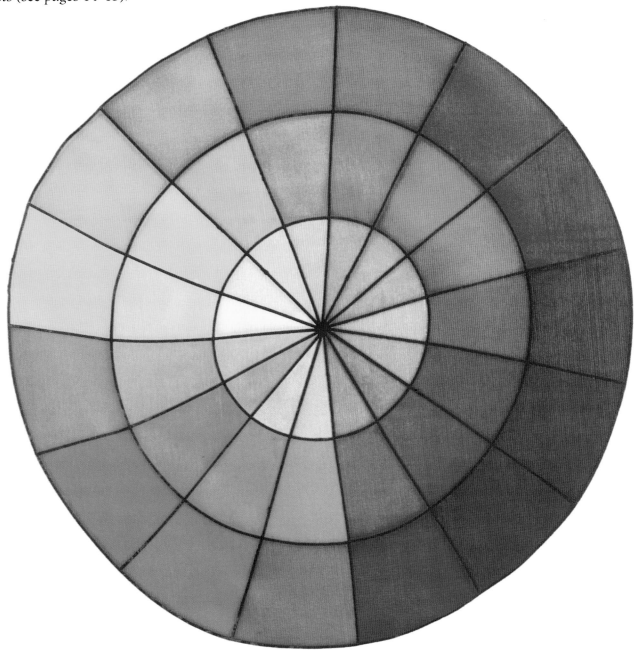

Subtle colours

If you mix complementary colours together you get wonderful ranges of browns, greys and even blacks! If you want to subdue or darken a colour, mix in its complementary colour. Try introducing a tiny bit at a time until you get the colour you want. Never use black – this simply deadens the colour.

Enhancing colours

If you paint complementary colours next to each other, they tend to enhance each other.

Jumping colours

If you make the tones of the complementary pair the same (so that neither one appears darker than the other when you look at them through half-closed eyes), they 'jump' against each other and can be used to create startling effects.

Petunias

The full vibrancy of silk dye colours only becomes apparent after steaming. Some pinks can become very strong, as these petunias show. It is always a good idea to test your colours before you use them for your final paintings – you will usually be delighted by the brilliance of the colours, but sometimes a subtle pink can turn into a shocking one!

16

Fixing dyes

When you have completed your painting, the dyes need to be steam-fixed so that they become colour-fast. Painted silk looks beautiful after steaming; the colours often become brighter and more intense, and the full sheen of the silk is restored. Even if you do not intend to wash your painting, it should still be fixed to make it light-fast.

Fixing involves wrapping the painted silk in cotton cloth or paper to prevent it from smudging, then exposing it to plenty of steam so that the dyes are able to combine with the silk fibres. Boiling when dip-dyeing serves the same purpose. Steaming with a steam iron is not sufficient to fix the dyes properly.

The fixing process is very simple and can be done in several different ways. The demonstration on page 18 shows how to steam-fix in a bamboo steamer. Follow the procedure carefully to avoid mishaps. Remember you want plenty of steam – not water – to get into your roll of painted silk. Keep everything dry in preparation and do not put too much water into the pan as it can bubble up and splash the silk. Always keep silk steaming equipment separate from that used for food.

After steaming, rinse the silk in cold running water to remove any excess dye. If you have used clear water-based gutta, you then need to soak the silk for a few minutes in warm water to remove all traces of the gutta. Towel dry or short spin, then iron it while still damp to remove the creases and restore the sheen of the silk.

The demonstration on page 18 shows how to steam-fix in a bamboo steamer.

TIPS

If you have used salt in your painting, make sure all the grains are brushed off before steaming.

Water-based gutta sometimes sticks to the steaming cloth or paper. Soak the silk in cold water for a few minutes and the paper or cloth will drop away.

Steaming cloths can be washed and reused many times.

A Chinese bamboo steamer fitted over a saucepan makes a very effective and inexpensive steamer. It is better than a metal one because it does not build up condensation. Allow the steamer to dry thoroughly between steamings as it can become saturated. Steam for approximately 1–2 hours, depending on the weight of the silk.

A pressure cooker shortens the steaming time considerably (down to approximately ten minutes). Be careful not to block the safety valve with too large a bundle. Fill with about 2.5cm (1in) of water and turn the heat down low when it has reached pressure to prevent it from boiling dry.

If you are painting lots of silk, a professional steamer is a good investment. You can steam large paintings and long lengths of silk in it. There are several different types – stove-top steamers are laid horizontally across a cooker, and the upright model shown here has a built-in electric element. Steam for approximately two hours, depending on the weight of the silk.

1. Cut a piece of clean, dry cloth (thin cotton sheeting is ideal) approximately 10cm (4in) bigger all round than the piece of silk that you want to steam. Lay the silk flat in the middle of the cloth and smooth out any creases. Roll up the cloth and silk loosely.

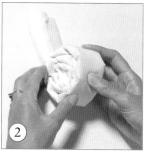

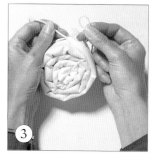

2. Coil the roll to make a snail-like bundle.

3. Secure the bundle with string. Tuck in the loose ends of the string to make a neat package.

4. Cut four circles of kitchen foil to fit inside the steamer. Place two circles in the bottom of the steamer, put the bundle on top, and then place the remaining two circles of foil on top of the bundle. Smooth down the foil over the sides of the bundle to make an umbrella shape – this will prevent condensation from dripping on to the bundle.

5. Fill a saucepan one-third full of boiling water. Place the steamer on top of the saucepan then place the lid on the steamer. Steam for 1–2 hours depending on the size of the silk. If you have to top up the water level during this time, use boiling water. When the silk is steamed, unwrap it and rinse it in cold running water to remove any dye residue.

How to start

There are lots of different ways of approaching flower painting on silk. Here are just some of them!

Working from designs

If you have no artistic experience or lack confidence in your creative abilities, you can use the linear designs in this book or work from tracings of photographs. You can transfer the designs on to silk using a soft graphite pencil, an autofade marker, gutta or outliner. If you trace from a photograph, remember that you need not copy it exactly as it is. The design may be improved by adding an extra flower, or leaving out a leaf! Use a photocopier to enlarge to the size you want. You can then enjoy the painting process without the anxiety of feeling you have to be able to draw first!

Working from photographs

Some flower painters like to work from photographs because flowers move and change as you paint them, and sometimes wither before the painting is finished. Photographs can also provide plenty of inspiration during the winter months, when there are not so many flowers around to paint. You can find beautiful photographs in gardening books and flower catalogues, or better still, take your own. This way you will have had the chance to study the real flowers and therefore have a deeper understanding of their growth and structure.

Working from real flowers

I prefer to work from real flowers. Before I start a painting, I make graphite pencil drawings in line and tone, or I use coloured pencils – this helps me to understand each flower's form and structure. Through drawing, I begin to simplify and clarify what I want to say about the flowers in my painting. I try to capture the 'essence' of each flower.

Before beginning to draw, it is a good idea to study the flower closely for a few minutes. Turn it round and examine the formation of the petals, the way the leaves grow out of the stem, how the buds open – all the details unique to that flower. When you feel you are beginning to understand it, make a simple line drawing on a large sheet of paper. Follow the edges of the flower,

The Finished Lily Project

This crepe de chine lily painting has been made up into a cushion cover. It uses gold metallic outliner as a resist and a bold, complementary colour scheme. The petals are painted in blended oranges and reds and over-painted with violet to shade them.

Lily cushions

These sumptuous silk crepe de chine cushions show three different colourways of the lily design featured in this chapter.

Oleanders

I love seeing oleanders in bloom in Mediterranean countries. They are often planted as flowering hedges by the roadside and against walls. They come in all shades of pink, crimson and creamy white. The flowers have a delicious scent and the leaves are dark and spear-shaped.

USING GUTTA RESIST

The most common resist used in silk painting is gutta. Traditional gutta is spirit-based. It is a liquid latex rubber which is totally water-repellent and forms an excellent resist. It can only be removed from the silk by dry-cleaning fluids. For this reason, many silk painters prefer to use the more modern water-based guttas which can be washed out of the silk after fixing.

There is some confusion as to the difference between 'gutta' and 'outliner' and manufacturers do not always agree on terminology. I tend to use the term 'gutta' for a resist which is clear or coloured with dye, and is removed from the silk after fixing, leaving a line which cannot be felt in the silk. I use the term 'outliner' for resists which are heavily pigmented with colour or metallic powders and can still be felt in the silk after washing.

Clear water-based gutta is used for this project. It is applied with a gutta bottle fitted with a gutta nib to achieve fine, even resist lines. Gutta can also be applied from a tube, but I find the nozzle on the tube tends to make a cruder line.

— YOU WILL NEED —

Frame, 37 x 43cm (14½ x 17in)

Three-point silk pins

Silk crepe de chine

Dyes: violety red, orangey red, orangey yellow, greeny blue, violety blue

Gutta, gutta bottle and nib

Round brushes, Nos. 6 and 8

3B or charcoal pencil or autofade marker

Board

1. Pin up the silk and trace the design very lightly (see page 23) with a pencil or an autofade marker. Remove the paper design and apply the gutta carefully over the traced design. Make sure the gutta penetrates through to the back of the silk and check that there are no gaps or breaks in the resist line. Allow the gutta to dry.

The oleander design

Enlarge by 315% for a full-size pattern

2. Mix your colours, then paint the flowers one at a time using a No. 6 brush. Begin by applying a light pink to the edges of the petals, then work in a mid tone. Finally, add a deep pink to the centre of each flower. Blend the tones into each other (see page 23).

3. Paint the leaves one at a time in tones of green. Begin with a light tone at the tip of the leaf then gradually blend in deeper tones to achieve shading. Paint the stems in a mid-green.

4. Add touches of dark pink to the stems then paint the flower centres yellow.

5. Paint in the background in a very dark bluey grey using a No. 8 brush. Leave to dry. Steam-fix before washing out the gutta with warm water.

Opposite

The Finished Oleander Project

These oleanders are outlined with clear gutta and the colours are carefully blended to create gradations of tone in the flowers and leaves. The dark background gives the painting an oriental look.

Peonies

This painting was inspired by some gorgeous peonies which were growing in my garden. The flowers were drawn straight on to the silk using spirit-based gutta – a good discipline to get you to really observe! Overpainting was used to build up darker edges around the petals and leaves.

Christmas rose

I have a large pot of Christmas roses outside my back door. It is always a delightful surprise to see their strong buds pushing up through the soil in mid winter. Their greeny white flowers are exquisite, each with a complex arrangement of fragile stamens. They withstand gales and snow, and lift the spirits on bleak winter days.

USING CLEAR GUTTA OVER A PAINTED BACKGROUND

The subtle colouration in the line work in this project is achieved by painting the silk with tints of green before outlining the leaves with gutta. This means that when the clear gutta is removed after fixing, some of the linework is white (around the flowers) and the rest is light green. This technique can be used in successive layers of painting so that the lines blend in with the colours used in the design or are 'hidden' (as in the flowers in this project). I have also incorporated the technique of painting on to damp silk (see page 49) in this project.

YOU WILL NEED
Frame, 43 x 43cm (17 x 17in)
Three-point silk pins
Silk habotai
Dyes: orangey yellow, greeny yellow, orangey red, greeny blue, violety blue
Round brushes, Nos. 1, 6, 8 and 10
Mop brush
Gutta, gutta bottle and nib
3B or charcoal pencil
Hairdryer
Board

The Christmas rose design
Enlarge by 375% for a full-size pattern

1. Pin the silk to your frame and trace the design with a pencil. Outline only the flower heads and buds with gutta, making sure that each section is contained. Trace over the stems of the stamens with gutta and apply a line around the outer edge of the border. Allow to dry.

TIP

You can use either spirit- or water-based gutta for this project. If you use spirit-based gutta you can blend straight over the stamens in step 2. Water-based gutta will stain or dissolve if painted over, so you must paint round it carefully.

2. Mix your colours, then use neat orange and yellow dye to paint in the stamen heads. Apply the dye in little dots using a No. 1 brush. Dry the dots with a hairdryer as you work to prevent them from spreading. Seal each stamen head with a dot of gutta.

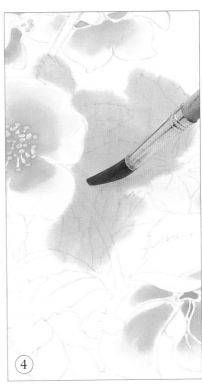

3. Use a No. 8 brush to dampen the flowers and buds with water. Blend a little light yellowy green into the petals, leaving the outer edges and tips white. Introduce a darker tone of green towards the centres of the flowers.

4. Dampen the rest of the silk with water. Use a mop brush for large areas and a No. 6 brush to work carefully around the flowers. Use a No. 10 brush to blend a yellowy green over the leaves and around the border.

5. While the silk is still damp, blend bluey green into some of the leaves and paint an edge of pink around the border. Leave to dry.

6. Outline the leaves, stems and border with gutta. Leave to dry. Overpaint the leaves using a No. 8 brush and shades of green and a little pink. Use the same pink to indicate the stems.

7. Paint the background dark green. Use a No. 10 brush for large areas, and a No. 6 for the spaces between the leaves and flowers.

TIP

To achieve an even background, paint back and forth along the damp spreading edge, overlapping it a little each time. Avoid going back over the wash as it starts to dry.

Opposite

The Finished Christmas Rose Project

The picture in the top right is the finished painting. It is built up in stages, using clear gutta applied over white silk and also over areas which have been painted. In this way the resist lines become less obvious and blend more subtly with the leaves, as shown in the large detail. In some areas, the resist lines are completely concealed.

The Finished Jasmine Project

The white jasmine flowers and the dense green foliage in this painting are achieved using successive layers of wax to resist the dye washes. Batik veining can be added to the leaves or flowers (see top right) by unpinning the silk and pinching the wax to crack it, then repinning and applying the dye.

41

Orchids

I find orchids fascinating. I am intrigued by their exotic shapes, strange colours and peculiar markings. They have evolved marvellously complex flower structures, cleverly designed to attract and sometimes trap insects, which ensures pollination.

USING WAX WITH A TJANTING

In this project the resist lines are made with hot wax applied with a tjanting to produce flowing outlines which are worked over a pre-painted background. When the flowers have been painted, the details are added to the petals with a fine brush, using a hairdryer to stop the dye spreading.

The orchid design
Enlarge by 420% for a full-size pattern

YOU WILL NEED

Frame, 49 x 44cm
  (19 x 17½in)
Three-point silk pins
Silk habotai
Dyes: violety blue, orangey
  red, greeny yellow
Round brushes, Nos. 1 and 6
Foam brush, 2.5cm (1in)
Mop brush
Wax and wax pot
Tjanting
Charcoal pencil
Paper towelling
Iron and old newspaper
Water mister
Gutta, gutta bottle and nib
Hairdryer
Board

42

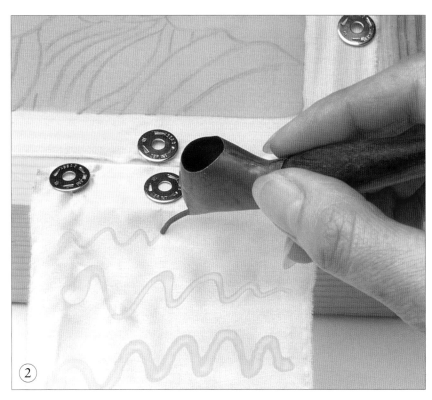

1. Pin the silk on to your frame and draw a line of gutta around the edge of it. Leave to dry. Trace the design with a charcoal pencil. Mix up your colours then use a water mister to dampen the silk. Use a mop brush to blend patches of pale pinks, oranges and greens to cover the silk. Re-tension the silk if necessary. Leave to dry thoroughly.

2. Heat up the wax and place the tjanting into it to heat up. Fill the tjanting then test the temperature of the wax by drawing the spout across a piece of spare silk. The wax should flow freely to form a dark transparent line. If the wax bubbles on the silk or spreads, it is too hot. If it forms a broken or white line it is too cool.

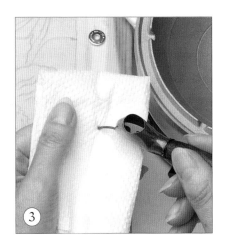

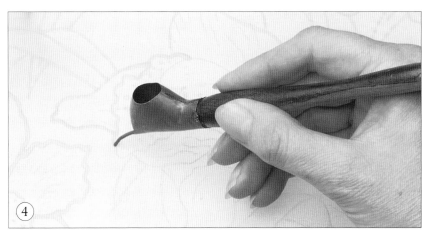

3. Carefully wipe the bowl of the tjanting and block the spout with paper towelling as you move across from the wax pot to the silk – this will prevent the wax from dripping on to your work.

4. Place the spout on the silk and trace over the design lines with wax, but do not outline the patterns in the petals. As soon as the wax ceases to flow freely from the spout, tip it back into the pot and refill it. Check the lines carefully and use the wax to fill in any breaks.

5. Use a No. 6 brush to paint the flowers in various blended shades of pink and green. Introduce darker tones as you work towards the centre of each flower.

6. Paint the flower centres, using blended tones of yellow, green and pink.

7. Paint the leaves and stems in various shades of green. Use dark tones to shade the underside of each leaf.

8. Use soft browns to paint in the orchid bulbs. Work green into the centres. Leave the silk to dry thoroughly.

9. Use a No. 1 brush to add tiny dark red spots and lines to the petals. Dab the brush on paper towelling to remove surplus colour as you work, and dry with a hairdryer to prevent the colour from spreading (be careful not to melt the wax as you do this).

10. Paint blended greens into the bottom half of the background. Leave the silk to dry. Iron out the wax between sheets of old newspaper (see page 40) before steam-fixing.

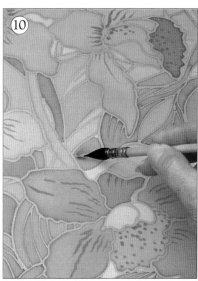

The Finished Orchid Project

These subtly coloured orchids are outlined with a resist of hot wax applied with a tjanting – a traditional Javanese batik tool. I have used muted pinks and greens to convey a steamy tropical atmosphere.

47

Daffodils

I love to see drifts of wild daffodils growing in dappled sunlight under trees and in long grass, and find few sights as cheering as beds of golden daffodils in parks and gardens in springtime. My seaside garden is rather wind-blown, so I grow the beautiful miniature varieties which withstand rough weather and come up faithfully year after year.

The Finished Daffodil Project
An impression of daffodils in spring sunlight is achieved in this painting by applying the colours directly on to damp silk. The dyes dry with a soft 'out of focus' look.

PAINTING ON DAMP SILK

When you paint on damp silk, the colours seem to spread less than on dry silk because the fibres are already saturated with water and there is nowhere for the dye to go. The painting dries with a soft, blurred 'out of focus' look. You can achieve excellent colour blending on damp silk because the dyes take longer to dry. Usually, more definition can be achieved on heavier silks than on finer ones. Experiment with different silks and try varying the degree of dampness to discover the many exciting effects that can be achieved.

This project is completed in one go before the silk has time to dry. You can use this method as a preliminary stage of a painting, before going on to employ other techniques in it.

The daffodils are freepainted, but I suggest that you place the design underneath the silk and use this as a guide while you paint. Work in a cool room so the silk does not dry too quickly and you do not have to paint too fast! Remember to work darker shades for the flowers in the foreground and lighter tones for the more distant ones.

The daffodil design
Enlarge by 870% for a full-size pattern

YOU WILL NEED

Frame, 49 x 43cm (19 x 17in)
Three-point silk pins
Silk crepe georgette
Dyes: greeny yellow, orangey yellow, violety blue, greeny blue, violety red
Round brush, No. 8
Water mister
Gutta, gutta bottle and nib
Polythene
Board

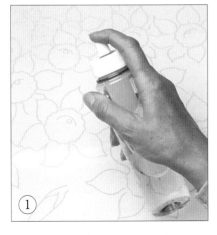

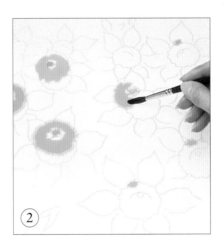

1. Pin the silk on to your frame. Lay a piece of polythene over the design to protect it, then place it underneath, but not touching, the silk. Draw a line of gutta around the edge of the silk. Leave to dry. Spray the silk lightly and evenly with water.

2. Mix your colours. Using the design as a guide, paint the stamens light yellowy green and use orangey yellow for the trumpets.

3. Blend a little orange into each trumpet to give them depth then paint the petals greeny yellow.

49

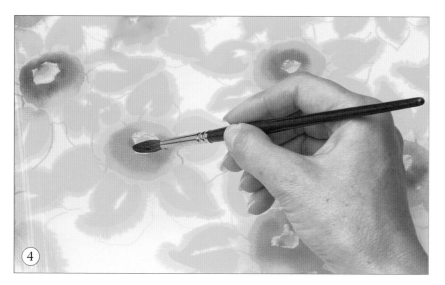

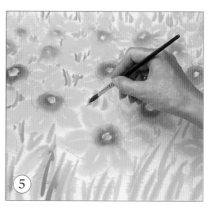

4. Blend a little violet into the foreground flower trumpets to add further depth.

5. Paint the leaves in light and mid greens. Use longer brushstrokes in the foreground and shorter ones in the distance.

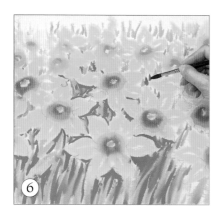

6. Fill in the spaces between the leaves with a darker bluey green. Use the colour sparingly when working the leaves in the distance.

7. Paint the sky using violety blue then use this same sky colour here and there between the flowers and leaves. Blend further violet into the flower heads in the foreground to add shade. Leave to dry then steam-fix.

TIP

Leave crepe georgette and chiffon to dry naturally – do not dry with a hairdryer as this spoils the dye surface and makes watermarks. Other silks can be gently dried with a hairdryer when the colours have merged as much as you want them to.

Opposite
Daffodil scarf
This long silk georgette daffodil scarf uses the same method of painting on damp silk as shown in the project.

Mallows

Annual mallows seed themselves and grow into bushy hedges covered in glossy pink flowers each summer. I photographed some mallows a while ago, and painted this textile design using the photographs for reference. I wanted to capture the delicacy of the sugar-pink blooms and the contrast of this colour against the lush garden foliage.

PAINTING ON DRY SILK

This project is painted directly on to silk without preliminary drawing. Mallows are a simple shape so they are ideal for the technique of painting without resists (more complex shapes can be more difficult to achieve due to the nature of the spreading dyes). The flowers are painted first, using a little colour blending on damp silk, and they are then dried. The foliage is added in small dabs of overlapping greens. Remember that dye spreads very freely on dry silk and in this project there are no resist lines to contain the spread – therefore, do not apply the green too generously or your flowers will be engulfed by the colour! The greens should spread only slightly across each other and across the edges of the pink flowers, to create ragged edges.

There is no pattern for this project, but you should draw in the flowers very roughly using an autofade marker. The autofade marker lines act as a temporary guide to the positioning of the flowers and they will dissolve away as soon as you paint over them.

The veins of the leaves and petals are worked using light, quick strokes and a fairly dry brush. It is a good idea to practise on a spare piece of silk before you start.

YOU WILL NEED

Frame, 36 x 42cm (14 x 16½in)
Three-point silk pins
Silk habotai
Dyes: violety red, violety blue, greeny yellow
Round brush, No. 8
Rigger brush, No. 4
Hairdryer
Gutta, gutta bottle and nib
Paper towelling
Autofade marker

Opposite

The Finished Mallow Project

These shiny pink mallow blooms are painted directly on to dry silk habotai. It takes a little practice to judge how far the dyes will spread – a hairdryer becomes a useful friend for stopping the colours in mid flow!

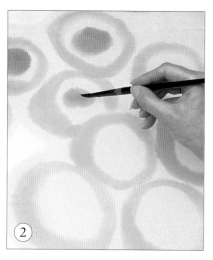

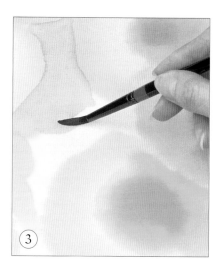

1. Pin the silk on to your frame then draw a line of gutta around the edge of it. Leave to dry. Use an autofade marker to roughly sketch the position of the flowers. Mix your colours, then use a No. 8 brush to paint water into one of the circles. Outline the circle with light pink. Repeat, painting in each flower one at a time.

2. While the dye is still damp, paint deep pink into the centre of each flower. Soften the edges on one side of each bloom, making sure that you retain a white area of silk – this will make the flowers look glossy. Dry evenly with a hairdryer.

3. Paint around each flower using the lightest green. Allow the colour to shape the wavy edge of the petals. Dry with a hairdryer.

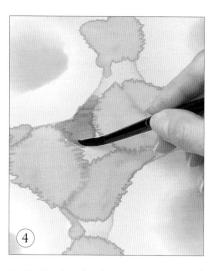

4. Paint in the leaves using mid greens. Dry with a hairdyer as you work. Introduce some dark green to add depth to the foliage and to define the leaves further. Again, dry with a hairdryer.

5. Use a No. 4 rigger brush and dark green to paint veins along some of the leaves.

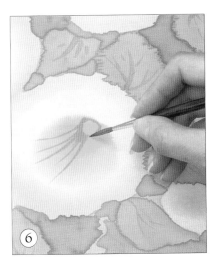

6. Use the same method as in the previous step to paint violety red veins on the flower petals. Carefully work in a dark red shadow in the centre of each flower. Leave the stamens unpainted. As you work, use the hairdryer to stop the colours spreading. When dry, steam fix.

TIP

When painting veins, dab excess dye on to paper towelling before you touch the brush on the silk. This will avoid too much colour flooding in.

Dandelion, petunia and hibiscus scarves

These floral scarves are painted on dry crepe georgette. A little clear gutta is used to give definition to the centres. When working on transparent silks like crepe georgette and chiffon, do not use a hairdryer – let the dyes soak in and dry naturally.

Tulips

I had an old friend who kept a beautiful cottage garden next to
my studio. He was a traditional, old-fashioned gardener
who grew vegetables and flowers alongside each other.
Every season his flower beds held new delights. One spring
he had beautiful cream tulips growing amongst rich red and
gold wallflowers. The bed was edged with forget-me-nots
and deep blue hyacinths. In the mornings, the sun filled the
tulips with light, making them float like moons above a sea of
colour. The beautiful combination of colours and textures was
the inspiration for this project, and I worked from a coloured
pencil sketch I made at the time.

PAINTING WITH BROKEN COLOUR

This project uses the technique of applying little dabs of colour on
to dry silk to create the effect of a mass of flowers around the
tulips. The tulips are painted first, then sealed with wax to
define them and to stop the other colours spreading into them.
It can be difficult to apply gutta on heavy silks such as crepe de
chine so that it forms an effective resist, so wax is a better
choice for this silk. Before you begin, you will need to heat up
the wax in a wax pot.

The broken colour technique is also very effective for
paintings on silk velvet and other heavier silks. It produces an
effect similar to that of pointillism – a technique developed by
Seurat in the 1880s, which used dots of colour which, when
viewed from a distance, would mingle and harmonise to give the
effect of sparkling light.

Opposite

Orange tulips

*These bold orange tulips are a variation of the project piece
shown on pages 60–61. They are painted on to dry crepe de chine
without the use of wax. The result is free, informal-looking flowers
with ragged edges. The background is textured with small dabs of
broken colour in complementary tints.*

YOU WILL NEED

Frame, 50 x 42cm
(19½ x 16½in)

Three-point silk pins

Silk crepe de chine

Dyes: orangey red, greeny
yellow, orangey yellow,
violety blue

Round brush, No. 8

Wax brush, No. 8 (with a good
point)

Wax and wax pot

Charcoal pencil

Water mister

Gutta, gutta bottle and nib

Paper towelling

Hairdryer

Iron and old newspaper

Board

The tulip design
Enlarge by 425% for a full-size pattern

1. Pin the silk on to your frame.
Draw a line of gutta around the
edge and leave to dry. Trace
the design on to the silk very
lightly using a charcoal pencil.
Mix your colours, then spray
the silk evenly with water.
Freely paint over the tulip
heads with light yellow using a
No. 8 brush. The colour will
spread slightly beyond the lines
at this stage.

2. While the silk is still damp, use a deeper yellow to shade around
the edge and into the centre of each flower. Dry with a hairdryer.

58

4. Brush over the flower heads with the darker yellow to fill in the gaps between the petals. Wipe off any surplus dye from the wax with paper towelling before it dries. Do not worry if a little dye seeps into the surrounding silk.

3. Wax over each flower head using a No. 8 wax brush. Leave spaces between the petals, using the design lines as a guide. Do not wax over the stems.

5. Paint over the stems with a light green. Add a little darker green under the flower head while the silk is still damp. You can dry the stems gently with a hairdryer as you work, to stop the green spreading too far, but be careful not to melt the wax. Leave to dry then wax over the stems and over the gaps between the petals to seal them.

6. Paint in the mass of wallflowers and forget-me-nots in little dabs of colour. Dry gently with a hairdryer as you work, to stop the dots spreading into each other. Build up the colours and tones, adding darker colours to increase the sense of depth in the foliage. Iron out the wax between sheets of newspaper (see page 40), then steam-fix.

The Finished Tulip Project

Wax is used to mask and define the pale yellow tulips in this painting. The mass of wallflowers and forget-me-nots are painted freely on to dry silk with small brushstrokes of colour.

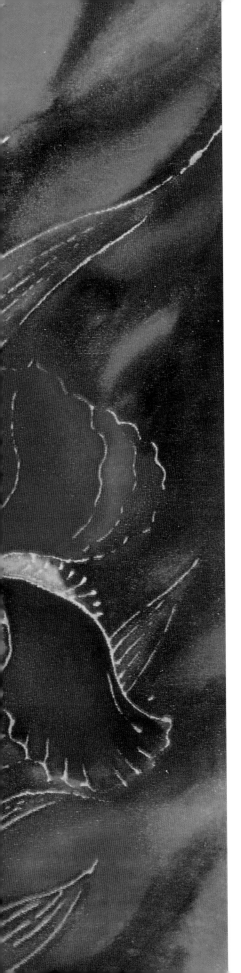

Irises

Painters have always loved irises, especially the large bearded varieties which grow in spreading clumps. They have dramatic fans of broad leaves, and tall stems which bear silky, fabulously-patterned flowers. They can be seen in a range of amazing colours – from delicate pinks, blues and lilacs to warm apricots, yellows and strangely speckled bronzes. I love the rich velvety purple ones with 'beards' like bright yellow, fluffy caterpillars.

The Finished Iris Project

You can achieve stunning effects on silk velvet. The pile produces very rich colours which shimmer in the light. In this painting of purple bearded irises, the outlines have been etched to give the flowers some definition and to reduce colour spread.

63

ETCHING ON SILK VELVET

This project is worked on silk/viscose velvet as the fabric is so reminiscent of the texture of the irises. Resists are not very effective on velvet due to the thickness of the pile, so the linear design has been etched out of the velvet pile using a special paste which can be purchased from silk painting suppliers and some craft shops. It works well on silk/viscose velvet, as it burns out the cellulose viscose pile, leaving the silk backing intact.

In this project, the outlines of the irises and some of the leaves are etched out. The etched lines give the painting some linear definition and a slightly 'quilted' appearance. They also help to stop the dyes spreading into adjoining areas during painting. The lines only act as a partial barrier however, so some colour blending does occur, which tends to enhance the quality of the painting.

Read through the project carefully before you begin and practise applying the gel on a spare piece of velvet and then ironing it. Do not set the iron too hot and do not iron for too long or you will turn the lines of etching gel black and burn holes in the velvet.

WARNING

Etching gel must be used with care and in a well-ventilated area. Always follow the manufacturer's instructions carefully and wear plastic gloves when working with it.

YOU WILL NEED

Frame, 47 x 50cm
(18½ x 19½in)

Stenter pins

Silk/viscose velvet

Dyes: violety blue, violety red, orangey yellow, greeny yellow, greeny blue

Etching gel

Round brush, No. 12

Autofade marker

Plastic gloves

Iron

Hairdryer

Board

The iris design

Enlarge by 370% for a full-size pattern

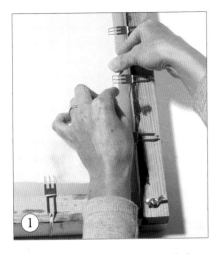

TIP

You may find it easier to apply a steady line of etching gel if you support your wrist on a yardstick or a piece of flat wood laid across the frame. Start in the top left-hand corner (if you are right-handed) and work your way down. This will prevent you from smudging the lines.

1. Loop stenter pins around the frame and through the elastic bands. Ensure that the velvet is pile side down, then hook the pins on to the edge of the fabric.

2. Trace the design using an autofade marker. Remove the design and board. Outline the design with etching gel, applied in the same way as you would gutta. Dry the gel with a hairdryer.

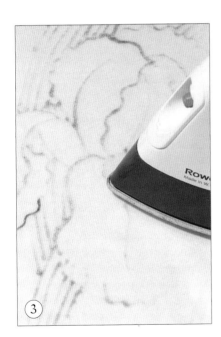

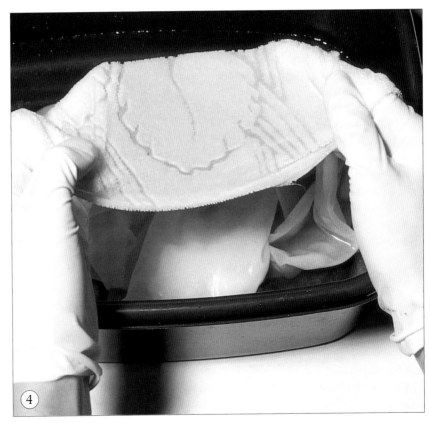

3. Remove the silk from the frame. Place it pile side down on your ironing board and carefully iron it using a dry iron on the silk/wool setting. Continue ironing until the lines change to a light brown colour and become brittle.

4. Rinse the velvet gently in water until the pile in the linear design drops away. Allow to dry.

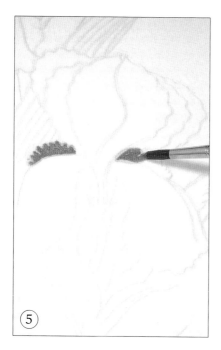

(5)

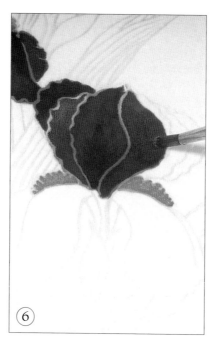

(6)

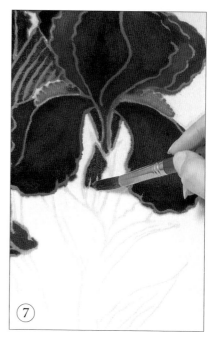

(7)

5. Pin the silk back on to your frame, pile side up. Mix your colours, then paint the flower stamens yellow using a No. 12 brush. Dry with a hairdryer to stop the dye spreading.

6. Paint the iris petals in blended violets and blues, leaving a margin around the stamens to allow for the spread of the dyes. Dry the area around the stamens to stop the colours spreading across into the yellow.

7. Paint the leaves and stems using bright and dull greens.

8

8. Paint violet into areas of the background to suggest distant buds and petals, and work dark tones between and around some of the leaves to create depth. Blend bright and dull greens into the rest of the background. Leave the velvet to dry thoroughly. Unpin the velvet, then steam-fix using two layers of cloth or steaming paper to absorb surplus dye. Rinse in cold running water, short spin then line- or tumble-dry for a short time.

TIP

Velvet can be ironed while still slightly damp to increase the sheen. Use the iron on a silk setting and press the pile in the direction of the nap (as if you were stoking a cat!).

Purple and gold irises
Wonderfully sumptuous effects can be achieved on velvet using the etching technique and a rich palette of colours. It is important to always mix and blend your colours well when working on silk velvet.

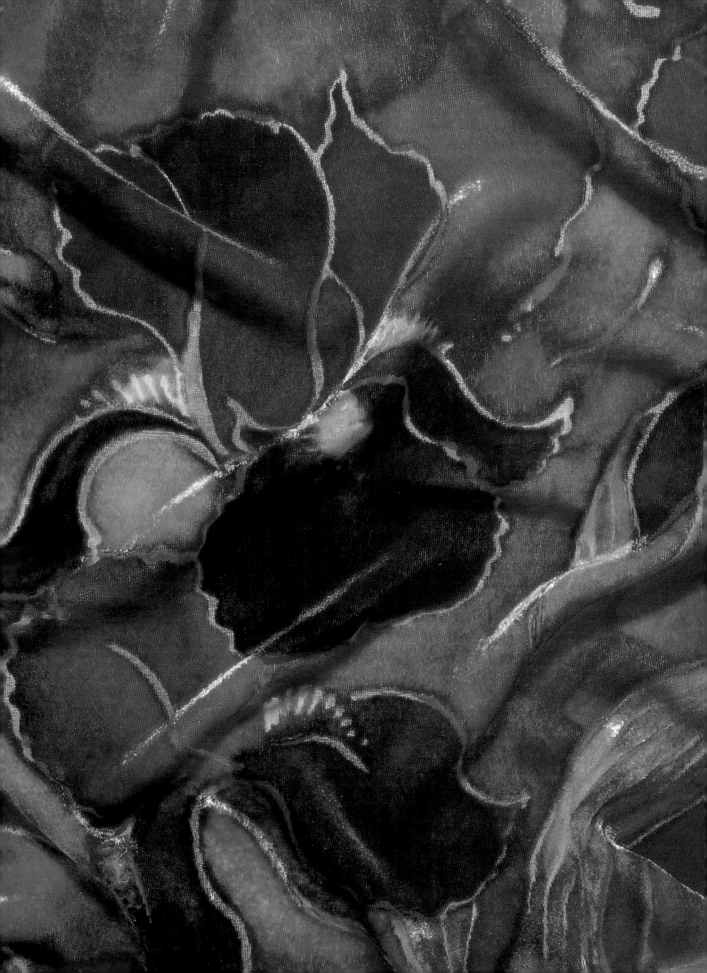

Amaryllis

Amaryllis are autumn-flowering bulbs native to South Africa, with pink, white or crimson trumpet-shaped flowers. You can grow a bulb in a pot on a window ledge. First a large shoot emerges which forms into a few large strap-shaped leaves. Later, a stout stem pushes up, topped with buds which open into a glorious crown of spectacular flowers – perfect for painting!

USING DIFFUSING MEDIUM

Diffusing medium can be mixed with the dyes to help them spread evenly. It can also be used to push the dye around on the painted silk to produce interesting marks and textures. This is a technique unique to silk painting, and it can be used to create many wonderful effects in flower painting – from ribbed leaves and layered petals to speckled and spotted foliage. Some painters use pure alcohol, water, or a mixture of both for this technique.

Lighter weights of silk tend to produce better results and some dyes 'move' better than others, so test your colours and silks before you begin.

YOU WILL NEED

Frame, 45 x 45cm (17½ x 17½in)

Three-point silk pins

Silk crepe georgette

Dyes: orangey red, violety blue, greeny blue, orangey yellow

Round brush, No. 10

Rigger brush, No. 4

Polythene

Gutta, gutta bottle and nib

Water mister

Diffusing medium

Hairdryer

Gold outliner

Polythene

The amaryllis design

Enlarge by 385% for a full-size pattern

68

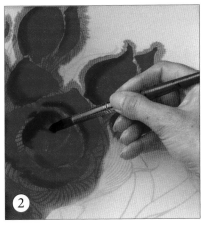

2. Blend yellow into the right-hand side of some of the petals to begin to create tone. Blend mid-violet into the left-hand side of the petals, and use dark violet for the flower centres.

TIP

Do not paint right up to the true edges of the petals and leaves. Leave the blues and violets to spread up to the wet red and green areas and allow the colours to merge where they meet.

---

1. Follow step 1 of the Daffodil project (page 49) to begin. Mix your colours, then use a No. 10 brush to paint in the red amaryllis flowers. Try to leave a little space between each petal.

TIP

When dyes dry on silk crepe georgette, they can often look quite pale. You may find it easier to remove the pattern and work with a piece of black fabric or paper underneath so that the colours show up more clearly. If you do this, simply refer to the pattern for the position of the veins and stamens.

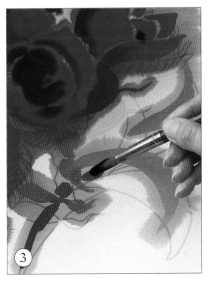

3. Paint in the leaves in shades of green and brown.

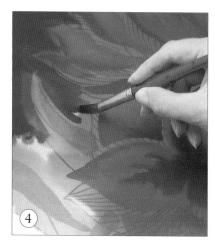

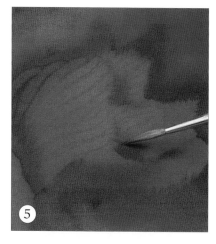

4. Paint the background using blended blues and violets. Use lighter tones of blue in the central areas between the flowers. Leave to dry naturally.

5. Use a No. 4 rigger brush to add streaks of diffusing medium to the petals to create veins. Control the spread of the diffusing medium by drying with a hairdryer when you are happy with the effect.

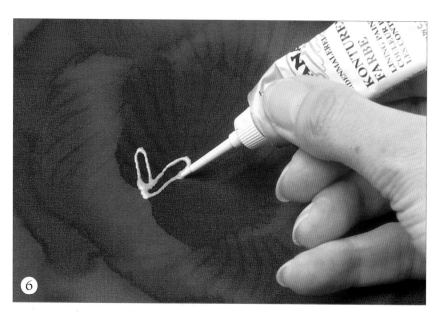

6. Draw in the stamens with metallic gold outliner. Leave to dry before steam-fixing.

The Finished Amaryllis Project

These rich red amaryllis blooms are on silk georgette. The petal veins are created by painting over the dry red dye with brushstrokes of diffusing medium. The diffusing medium drives back the dye to create light lines with dark edges. Metallic gold outliner is added as an ornate touch for the stamens when the rest of the painting is finished.

Hibiscus

I have a beautiful blue hibiscus in my garden which bursts into bloom in mid summer. The flowers are a marvellous shade of clear violet blue, flushed with crimson in the centres, and the stamens form little cream-coloured cones which extend from the flower centres. In certain lights, the blue flowers seem to glow against the bright green foliage.

The Finished Hibiscus Project

These stunning blue hibiscus flowers are painted on silk habotai treated with anti-spread medium. This controls the spread of the dyes and makes it more like painting on paper!

USING ANTI-SPREAD

In traditional Chinese painting and early European silk painting, the silk was treated with natural gums and starches so that the colours would not spread. This method can be used in modern silk painting to achieve effects similar to watercolour painting on paper, but with the advantage of being able to use the strong, pure colours that you get with dyes. Different ranges of silk dyes and paints are supplied with their own anti-spread medium. Alternatively, you can mix your own by adding water to thickener.

In this project the whole piece of silk is treated. You can, however, just treat certain areas of a painting, so that fine details such as veins in petals or leaves may be painted. Anti-spread can be painted over pre-painted areas too, although some dye disturbance will occur if the dyes have not been fixed. Anti-spread is washed out of the silk with warm water after steaming.

1. Pin the silk on to your frame. Trace the design very lightly with a charcoal pencil. Pour the anti-spread medium into a palette then paint it on to the silk evenly using a foam brush. Adjust the pins to re-tension the silk. Leave to dry.

The hibiscus design

Enlarge by 330% for a full-size pattern

73

2. Mix your colours, then use a No. 8 brush to paint the flowers one by one in blended tones of blue. Work carefully around the central stamens to leave them white. While the dye is still wet, blend pink into the base of the petals. Leave to dry.

3. Paint in the stamens using dots of creamy yellow, applied with the tip of the brush.

4. Add veining to the petals using undiluted dark red and the tip of the brush.

5. Paint in the leaves using various shades of green, starting with the lightest. Use a dark bluey green in the background to add depth to the foliage. Dry the silk then steam-fix it. Rinse the anti-spread out in lukewarm water to restore the soft handle of the silk.

Opposite

Poppies

Poppies, with their delicious colours and silky petals, are favourite subjects to paint on silk. This bed of poppies is painted on silk crepe de chine treated with anti-spread medium.

Poppies

A field of poppies is a wonderful sight but sadly one not often seen now, due to the use of pesticides and weed killers. However, even a verge of scarlet poppies beside a road turns heads and brings a moment of pleasure to passing motorists.

DISCHARGING WITH ILLUMINANTS

Discharging using illuminants is a method of bleaching out colour from a dyed fabric and replacing it with another colour. It is a way of achieving light or bright colours on a dark background. A reducing agent (discharge salt) is used to remove areas of colour. Illuminants (dyes which are unaffected by the reducing agent) are mixed with the discharge salt so that as one colour is bleached out, a new one takes its place. Water can be mixed with the illuminant to make a lighter colour.

Discharging materials are available from specialist silk painting suppliers. Also, experiment with your own dyes to discover which will discharge successfully. Remember to wear plastic gloves, and follow the manufacturer's instructions carefully.

YOU WILL NEED

Frame, 50 x 34cm (19½ x 13½in)

Stenter pins

Silk/viscose velvet

Round brushes, Nos 8 and 12

Dischargeable silk painting dyes: greeny blue, violety blue, greeny yellow

Illuminant: orangey red

Plastic gloves

Thickener

Discharge salt

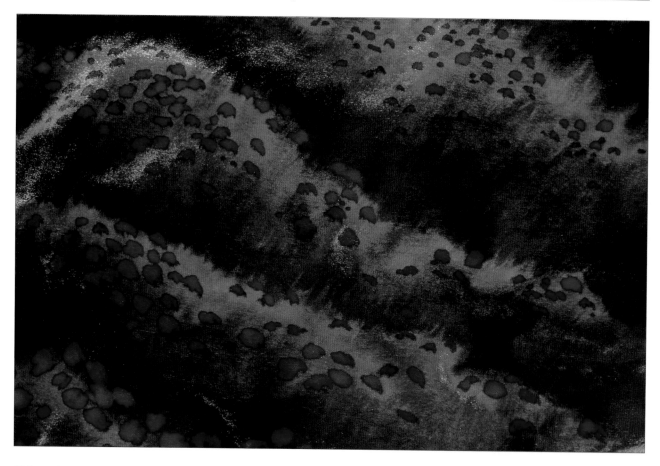

1. Wear plastic gloves to mix ¼tsp of discharge salt with 10ml of thickener. Stir until the salt has dissolved. Mix in 10ml of red illuminant. Test on a spare piece of silk to check the strength of the colour and the consistency of the paste – it should paint on easily and it should not spread.

2. Pin the silk, pile side up, on to the frame using stenter pins. Mix your colours, then paint the grassy background using a No. 12 brush. Begin with bands of light greens, worked in bold diagonal brushstrokes to suggest blades of grass.

3. Introduce darker greens to create the effect of patches of shadow in a grassy field. Leave to dry.

Opposite

The Finished Poppy Project

This painting on silk velvet features bright red poppies sharply defined against green grass. The poppies are added using discharging salt and a red illuminant, which means there is no need for a linear division of resist between the two colours.

4. Paint the poppies using a No. 8 brush and the red paste. The red looks dark on the silk at this stage. Leave to dry, then steam the silk in the usual way, using one or two extra layers of paper or cloth to absorb the surplus dye in the thickener.

Wild roses

Roses have been favourite subjects for painters and designers for centuries. There are wonderful old and new varieties of cultivated roses in many different colours and formations, but I always think there is something especially pleasing about the simple, delicate wild roses which grow in tangled profusion in the hedgerows in summer.

USING SALT

This project uses salt to create texture in the leaves. It is sprinkled on to the painted silk while the dye is still damp and patterns appear after a few minutes, as if by magic, and continue to increase until the silk is dry. The effect can be stopped at any time by gently drying with a hairdryer. Do not heap the salt on, as it will take out too much colour and spoil the patterning – use just a fine sprinkling. Flick off any grains from resist lines as they will filter the colour across and cause 'bleeds' into adjacent sections.

Lots of different types of salt can be used for this technique – fine cooking salt makes delicate texturing for small flowers or foliage, and coarse rock or sea salt produces bolder patterns which are ideal for larger leaves or backgrounds. An even-grain 'effect salt' is sold by silk painting suppliers.

YOU WILL NEED

Frame, 29 x 29cm (11½ x 11½in)

Three-point silk pins

Silk habotai

Dyes: greeny blue, violety blue, violety red, orangey yellow

Round brush, No. 8

Fine salt

Charcoal pencil or autofade marker

Gutta, gutta bottle and nib

Hairdryer

Board

The wild rose design

Enlarge by 520% for a full-size pattern

1. Pin up the silk. Trace the design and outline with gutta. Leave to dry. Paint the flowers and background. Leave to dry. Paint in the green leaves, working small areas at a time. While they are still damp, sprinkle on fine salt.

2. Leave for approximately one minute then dry the silk gently with a hairdryer. Brush off the salt with your hand to reveal the patterning. Ensure that all grains have been removed before steam-fixing the colours.

The Finished Wild Rose Design

I used the design above as the basis for a much larger piece – a section of which is shown here. Fine cooking salt was used to mottle the leaves.

Index